To my future husband...

With much love,

_____

Words capture a moment -
a story, a thought,
a feeling.
Let all of these moments
rest easy here until
your eyes may read them.

Date: /   /

I decided to start this journal because...

_____

_____

_____

_____

_____

_____

_____

_____

_____

_____

_____

_____

_____

_____

_____

_____

_____

_____

First, let me tell you about
who I am right now...
and who I hope to be.

Date: / /

Next, let me share
what I hope for you.

Date: /   /

Marriage is discovery.
I look forward to learning
how to love you.

Date: / /

This is what I have learned about love...

_____

_____

_____

_____

_____

_____

_____

_____

_____

_____

_____

_____

_____

_____

_____

We all face hardship.
Marriage gives a partner
through the ups and downs.
I will walk beside you
through the darkest nights
and rejoice with you in the
brightest days.

Date: / /

The presence of family,
the absence of family,
the love and loss,
hardship
and joyful times...
all may shape who we are.

Date: / /

Let me introduce you to my family...

_____

_____

_____

_____

_____

_____

_____

_____

_____

_____

_____

_____

_____

_____

_____

_____

_____

Our beliefs are a huge part of who we are. Let me tell you about mine.

Date: / /

Why I believe...

_____
_____
_____
_____
_____
_____
_____
_____
_____
_____
_____
_____
_____
_____
_____
_____
_____
_____

We all have fears.
I will stand beside you
against yours.
Together,
we will be strong.

Date: /   /

Let me share my heart...

_____

_____

_____

_____

_____

_____

_____

_____

_____

_____

_____

_____

_____

_____

_____

_____

_____

_____

*I am confident
you will be...*

Date: / /

Dear Future Husband,

I promise to...

Date: / /

The world is full of
wonderful places.
Someday, I hope we can
travel and see...

Date: / /

Traveling with a loved one is full of surprises...

_____

_____

_____

_____

_____

_____

_____

_____

_____

_____

_____

_____

_____

_____

_____

_____

I look forward to
conversations and
adventures with you.
Until then,
let me share a memory here
that is dear to my heart.

Date: /   /

I have waited patiently
for you.
Someday, I hope our
mornings can look like...

Date: / /

I'm looking forward to lots
of laughs together.

Date: / /

Some things that make me laugh...

_____

_____

_____

_____

_____

_____

_____

_____

_____

_____

_____

_____

_____

_____

*I hope we can make
the world a
better place together.
Here are some things I am
passionate about...*

Date: / /

My thoughts on
children,
a family,
our home...

Date: / /

I strive for
a life well-lived.
At the end of our lives,
I hope we will have...

Date: / /

I want to share
my life with you.
Let me share my...
happiest day.

Date: / /

I want to share
my life with you.
Let me share my...
saddest day.

Date: / /

I want to share
my life with you.
Let me share my...
Time of greatest growth.

Date: / /

I want to share
my life with you.
Let me share my...
Time I was angriest.

Date: / /

I want to share
my life with you.
Let me share my...
Time I was bravest.

Date: /   /

Enough about me...
Let me give you some
words of encouragement.

Date: / /

I never want to stop learning and growing. Here are some things I am learning that I look forward to sharing with you...

Date: / /

Let me share today
with you.

Date: / /

Until we can walk through each day together...

_____

_____

_____

_____

_____

_____

_____

_____

_____

_____

_____

_____

_____

_____

_____

_____

You are my treasure.
I will know you are the
one for me when...

Date: /   /

for when
I have found you...

To my dear
Future Husband...

Date: / /

For the night before

You are mine...

Date: / /

With all my love,

Made in the USA
Las Vegas, NV
25 July 2024

92903322R10069